The Healing Adagio . . .
A Love Symphony
In Five Parts

By Melony McGant
with Fellow Truth Seekers

Forward heart songs by

Deborah Ballard

and

H. Daniel Mujahid

AuthorHouse™
1663 Liberty Drive
Bloomington, IN 47403
www.authorhouse.com
Phone: 1-800-839-8640

First published by AuthorHouse   09/24/2011

ISBN: 978-1-4670-3816-4 (sc)

Printed in the United States of America

Any people depicted in stock imagery provided by Thinkstock are models, and such images are being used for illustrative purposes only.
Certain stock imagery © Thinkstock.

This book is printed on acid-free paper.

What Is Love to YOU?

For me, Love is not about money or power or things. Love is about smiles, kind words and hugs filled with appreciation.

Love is spoken and unspoken but lived through sharing acts of hope and support.

Love is comfort through the storms of life, and clearing the debris of disappointment and despair as I move forward with faith and a peaceful heart!

What is Love to YOU?

For My Mother

Betty J. Tilman,

and the birthing of

The Jackie Mullins

Good Neighbor Project . . .

May We All Be Inspired With Hope----
Re-membering and living as Good
Neighbors all over the Earth and
Throughout the Universe . . . .

For Our Children . . .

I can only hope that our enthusiasm and desire for goodness becomes more poignant and real each passing day.

May we learn to embody mercy and compassion for all so that all are safe and free to make good choices.

May we live our lives as a good neighbors in loving prosperous communities of respect and tolerance.

May we share our time together nurturing hearts and building strong peaceful, healing foundations of hope for children to explore and grow and share their many gifts with love.

Call Me A Dreamer!

The Healing Adagio

Beloveds,

Like forgiveness, healing can be embraced

as an Inward Adagio that begins slowly;

first with each breath of love.

Deep breathing allows for focus, clarity

and a connection with Divine Spirit.

The slow strengthening rhythm of adagio

moves through the body, as it becomes

the song of one blossoming in healing,

hope and illuminated with a deep, power faith!

Your Adagio then becomes a Loving Dance With G-d!

The Healing Adagio

Moving Forward Heart Songs are
written by Deborah Ballard and H. Daniel
Mujahid, along with Heart Songs from
James Aloway, Peter Andrews, Evens
Anozine, Gloria Brown, Tehuti Carter
Jones, Andrea Christofferson, Adrienne
Croix, Kay Dendy, Katherine Henry, Gayle
Hodnett Dobbs, Rev. Sedrick Gardner,
Sunil Gupta, Patricia Moore, Karen Piazza,
Pamela Patrick, Norbu Tsering,
and Dr. Glory Van Scott.

The Healing Adagio
Call and Response . . .

"Please publish a book with these timely and potent words to live by. I love and need them so much. Thank you again. Much love and peace to you!"

Pamela Patrick

"Reverend Melony McGant's written words of wisdom, inspiration and encouragement,—travel beautifully off the pages of her new book **The Healing Adagio**. The reader's eyes behold words of her truly universal spirit—which touches your heart, and gently rocks your soul.

Her timely messages of truth will gladden and uplift your day, and gladden and uplift your year!"

Dr. Glory Van Scott

The Healing Adagio . . .
A Love SymphonyIn Five Parts
Table of Contents

A Moving Forward Heart Song for The Healing Adagio . . .

"Man means Mind"

—Imam W. Deen Mohammed—

Although creation evolves, history tends to repeat itself. Today, the layperson is as qualified as the doctors of medicine, or the "judges" of society to describe the state of the world as "sick" and in dire need of healing, some even say exorcism . . . despite the fact that what we share through common endowment far outweighs our "plague-ful" differences.

In a wonderful way, this collection of works, **The Healing Adagio**, and its Author, **The Rev. Melony McGant**, bring both joy and understanding by outlining a circumspective detail of HOPE. For many these pages are sure to be a catalyst which supports your sense of responsibility in helping to remake the destiny of our children.

This "adage" alone highlights our need to restore respect for our sacred human core values, and our shared freedoms. In this way we, you and I, inherit the original acceptance for the very "Spirit of Mother", and Gratitude to Fathers" . . . **whose redemption is a debt we owe ourselves.**

H. Daniel Mujahid

A Moving Forward Heart Song for The Healing Adagio . . .

"Open The Healing Adagio at any page, feel the love, find the encouragement as it gracefully blesses your life journey!"

The Healing Adagio is a collection of inspirational writings full of Ancient Wisdom to encourage you in your life journey. Reverend Melony McGant has unselfishly allowed herself to be a vessel in which Divine Inspiration flows.

As I read this book, it became apparent that it is all about Love. Personally I realized that I needed to start with self-love. In acknowledging the Divine Presence of God within, I am able to love the wonderfully created "ME". In loving myself, I have forgiven myself; thereby I am able to easily love and forgive others.

Love is the driving force of the Universe and contains the Power to Heal. Through love, Forgiveness, Compassion and Mercy are easily found. In love there are no boundaries that separate only demonstrations that we are all connected. When everything in you may want to hold a grudge, point a finger or remember the pain, **The Healing Adagio** will remind you that the Divine within calls you to lay it aside and just love. Grief, pain, anxiety, uncertainty are transformed into something precious as Reverend McGant reminds us that love brings light to any situation no matter how difficult. **Open The Healing Adagio at any page, feel the love, find the encouragement as it gracefully blesses your life journey!**

Deborah Ballard

The Healing Adagio . . .

The One-dearful Reality

Love Is . . .

Love is the patience

that pours
like a waterfall
and offers us

understanding and clarity
so that we can see

throughout the vastness

of the universe—
the stars of hope that light the sky!

Learning Your Instrument

Life can be an Orchestra!
The Divine Conductor may call on you
to be a sax, a piano, a drum, a bell,
a violin, a flute, a cello, a trombone or a clarinet.
You may be any one of many instruments
that enjoys a passionate solo.

There is no time to audition.
We often must feel the rhythm
and follow the tune of love
with the divine orchestra.
Love is always presence and working in our lives.
No matter who we are, we all have the potential
to be instruments of divine love!

Rhythm of Love

When others have forgotten the rhythm of love,
it takes courage to live in divine truth.
All around us there are those who fear
embracing oneness. Still by being gentle,
genuine and generous, we are able to create
the melodies of hope.
Today re-member that you are supported
and loved.
Follow the Universal Conductor
within your heart.
Let the melody of your life be gentle, genuine
and generous, and filled with grace.
Have courage and live the divine truth of
your life in the Rhythm of Love.

Song of a Sinner

Love was all around me every day—
in the smiles of the children,
in the melody of a song,
in the dance of the trees blowing in the wind,
in the light of the moon,
in the warmth of the sun,
and even the roar of the ocean.

Love was before me everywhere.

But my ego needed control and in control,
I destroyed it all.

Then empty and alone, my heart became
broken and scattered throughout the Universe.

And in the emptiness of eons beyond time,
I was filled with the benevolent
mercy of our Creator.

It was then, beyond the desire
of my selfish ego that even me,
the worst of sinners
was forgiven and born again in Grace.

Having learned that lesson, now I am able to offer Only Love!

I Am ONE

Today Joy moves through me as I learn compassion and humility. I am ONE with all sentient beings . . . the sky, the clouds, the sun, the rain, the trees that sway and dance in the wind, and the birds that greet me in song.

I am One with the Spirit of Mother Theresa, Malcolm, Martin, John, and Edward as well as Ruth, Isaac, Joshua, Mary, Jesus, Khadijah, Mohammed, Shams, Buddha, Kuan Yin, Eva, Jackie, Kathryn, Maida and Sojourner Truth.

I am ONE with the woman suffering from breast cancer and the man suffering and dying from lung cancer and the woman in Afghanistan whose family was killed by a drone.

I am ONE with the homeless woman pushing the cart with all her worldly possessions and warning us of our greed though we don't often listen.

I am One with the Tibetan who was told by Chairman Mao that religion is poison and the Palestinian wandering, unable to return to his homeland.

I am One with the starving child of Sudan and the Israeli settler with a gun in his hand. I am One with every child born at this moment and the great-grandparents who are taking their last breath on this Earth Realm.

I am ONE with the artist struggling to show us the way and the politician disgraced in shame.
I am ONE with those who have awakened in love and those filled with fear.

Circumstances make no difference to me for I embrace the journey and see the Divine in those who may not see the Divine in themselves.

I Am ONE Cont

I am One with the President who needs more courage to say stop the killing everywhere and the Dalai Lama whom asks us to live in peace.

In my dreams the buffalo woman, the morning dove and the golden hawk guide me as my heart becomes filled with ancient prayers of all traditions.

I am One with the caterpillar and the butterfly.

I am One with the Buddhist, the Christian, the Jew, the Moslem, the Bahai, the Hindu, the Yoruba, the Janist, the Naturalist, the One who doesn't believe in God and the One Lost in their material identity and always needing more . . . .

Today Joy moves through me as compassion, humility and understanding become a way of life . . .

For in YOU, I See the Reflection of ME and Know WE ARE ONE.

Peace

Peace is possible when
we remember the magic of love
and re-connect to Divine Grace.

So many of you are living peace
and singing the song of peace.

How beautiful each of you are
as you create new chords
for a Universal Song.

All over the world you are awakening
and singing about a Loving Peace.
Thank you.

Please keep singing and
living the message of Peace.
You have opened the door
to the miracle realm.

All good is possible and probable
when we live with a Loving
Peace in Our Hearts!

Peace.

This is the Song and the Word of Love!

Beyond Doubt

Our Creator's love for us
is beyond reason,
and beyond doubt.

Throughout the universe
there are galaxies of love,
planets of compassion
and stars of hope.

When we learn to simply plant
and nurture the seeds of love,
then we too begin to grow
and live beyond doubt.

Beyond doubt . . .
Is the loving
Heart of Our Creator calling
on us to believe only in the
power of goodness . . .

Asking us to care for our Earth
as we embrace the harvest
of miracles and peace that
comes only through love!

Heaven On Earth

Come walk with me
into this magnificent valley
filled with greatness . . .
Smell the magnolias & cherry blossoms.

Walk with me
through the daffodils and daisies . . .
Feel free to pick a rose
and know that it's thorns
represent ages and ages of Divine wisdom.

Stop a moment.
Tenderly touch the dirt of our earth
and know that it is Mother
to fruits, vegetables, trees and flowers . . .
Living things.

As we move on in our discovery
select a rock or two along the way . . .
Cherish these rocks and know
that their firmness
truly represents the will of the Divine.

Do you hear the lilt of the wind
and the birds chirping
in delight of our presence?

Look what a glorious waterfall . . .
imagine yourself as a frog
jumping from a lily pad
and splashing into a clear pond.

Now gaze intently into the pool of life . . .
Permit our reflections to show merely Love . . .
For Love is the only weapon we need
to conquer the fear in our hearts.

Will you allow me to take your hand?
May we always walk together
in Heaven on Earth—feeling Divine Love?

Spirit Ramblings

My heart dreams often . . .
looking into the eyes of strangers
seeing love, feeling love.
For they are not strange to me.

Often it is a brother or sister,
maybe even a mother, a father
or a dear friend from a past life.
I wonder do they know me too
or are my soul ramblings vivid only to myself?

My thoughts are so intense,
viewing yesterdays and tomorrows
as if they are today.

The concept of time escapes me.
But come let us travel around the galaxy and share joy.
Our hearts know no limitations
for we can be One with the Divine through love.

'And what is love?' You ask.
Love is a rainbow or a smile glistening like a star at night.

Love is a storm readjusting & cleansing the earth
so that plants will grow
and we may feel even
the sizzle of an ant and know bliss.

Love is opening your heart
and feeling the wisdom of an oak tree
or the magical transformation of a caterpillar to a butterfly.

Love is walking along the shore,
your feet gently nestled in the sand
with ocean water caressing your legs
and the smell of a salt breeze kissing your face
as you watch the sun set or the moon rise
and ponder swimming with the dolphins.

Spirit Rambling Cont

Love is believing that ALL people
are gifts from the Divine
and knowing that each of us is related
and interconnected with every other sentient being.

Love is everything, everywhere.
Love is co-creating with the Divine.

'How do we co-create?' You ask.
Imagine that when your fingers tingle for no apparent reason
that That is the Divine teaching you, helping you to understand what it is
like when a flower blooms.

Or perhaps when you experience unexplainable tears of joy,
your heart is opening, expanding like a womb when a baby is being born.
And so on some level,
you too understand the bliss of motherhood.

You smile. That is good.
My spirit ramblings have often brought me much laughter.
Laughter can release fear and helps us understand one another. Laughter
is for me a desire for Grace,
A desire to reconnect with other souls.

My heart feels many thoughts around me.
Some are asking 'how can we co-create the bliss of love?'
'It is not possible.' You say.

Here is a question for You . . .
If it is possible to feel my heart beat
"boom ba ba ba boom ba boom ba ba ba boom",
is it because you remember love or is it the fear
that one you hold dear will leave again?

Do not answer, but muse in your heart.
Remember, it is time to forgive. Time only to love.

**Now come, let us travel together on our soul journey
back to Love, back to the Divine.**

Hello World. Welcome HOME!

Hello World!
This is a dinner invitation.

Come as you are!

Bring your joys and your sorrows.

Bring your hopes, your fears, your great success and desperate failures.

Bring your shadows of disappointment, envy and greed.
Nourishment and Transformative Healing awaits you!

Come as you are to the Home and Heart of Compassion.

Here, humility, understanding, forgiveness and gratitude is the food offered for your Soul.

As you taste each morsel,
your faith will blossom with hope and joy.

Welcome Home!
Only Love Can Prosper Here!

The Healing Adagio . . .

Heart Songs from Melony and Fellow Truth Seekers

I AM NOTHING

I am nothing.
I am everything and yet I am nothing . . .
just a tiny speck in the circle of life

a speck of love that grows
by reflecting joy to others.

I am nothing.
I am everything and yet I am nothing
as I travel through tunnels of despair
in search of peace.

I face fear.

It is the not knowing that hurts.
Who will I become if I am nothing?

I am nothing. How can I be everything?
The light guides me.

I learn to live
to walk in the light
of a rainbow and my nothingness
becomes everything as I awaken . . . .
learning to reflect beauty and joy.

I am nothing. I am everything
yet I am nothing . . . just a tiny speck
in the circle of life.

I am nothing.
I am everything . . .

Dreaming Dreams Too Wonderful To Dare Aloud

(Half Re-Membered Thoughts for Melony)

by James Aloway

There were days when it was difficult to imagine
That there would be a tomorrow after tomorrow;
or that my vision of yesterday
was clear enough to shine the path.

There were Mornings that came too soon
after work that seemed just through
with Sun light peeping between the cracks
in the torn window shade,
screaming the news
"It is time to start another day."

Just 10 more minutes and I will be fine . . . .

My back aches!
Oh Lord, help me through another day!
Did I pay the water bill?

None of this seemed
to make any sense back then,
though occasionally there was the Light.

Times when I could see
more than half remembered dreams
of Momma's crib songs
and Poppa's hope dream for me.

I met three Queens standing tall,
with shiny thought jewels
that sometimes blinded me.

Dreaming Dreams Too Wonderful To Dare Aloud
(Half Re-Membered Thoughts for Melony) Con't

They showed me the three mountains
I needed to climb.
Each mountain higher than the other,
all piercing the clouds.

Baby, my feet hurt!
Oh Lord, help me through another day!
When are they coming to turn the lights back on?

Standing on the curb and not lying on it
gives a different perspective on things.

I could see for miles, or at least down the street.

I can understand, believe . . . have Faith.

Folks heading west, while I'm moving East.
Cast a star in my eye, show me the way.

A King followed by a Queen and another Queen.
Cast a star in my eye,
show me the way—it's a new day,

Show me the way. I pray . . .
Oh Lord, help me Lord.

I pray . . .
Oh Lord, help me through another day!

James Aloway

Occupation: Volunteered Slavery in Corporate America **(a nod to Rahssan Roland Kirk—May he live on**). **Spiritual Path:** Seeker of Truth. **Dream for the World:** That we remember the dreams we had as children and that we love each other more each day!

Journey of the Heart

Melony,

Thank you for inviting me to be a part of your journey, a journey to the heart.

Work of this magnitude will allow us to step closer to the wisdom of emotions; the pleasantry of a new hello and the sorrow of never saying goodbye nor biding **A Dieu** . . .

Often I find your work to be apropos to my everyday life. There are times when I ponder if you're looking in. The loss of a dear friend, brother, sister, mother, father, daughter, son or even the one that got-away . . . can at times be so compelling that there are no possible way to express it.

Thank you for your wisdom and for giving a voice to emotions that we often fail to stop and ponder upon. I look forward to this great work that you are publishing. Not only am I anxious to read it, I can't wait to share it! Joy . . ."

Evens Anozine

On Loss

Many of us will experience great loss in our
lifetimes.

Those we love will leave.

We may lose our jobs or our homes.

We may lose our way or forget our dreams.

Loss teaches us acceptance and gratitude for what
remains.

Through deep self-reflection and faith,

we are able to embrace the pain,

honor our sacrifices and Move On!

Ultimately, every loss brings hope needing to be
nurtured with courage and allows us to cherish the
gift of re-membering

our loving purpose and good dreams.

"On Loss"

"This is one of my favorite messages from you because it encourages us to find meaning in pain, suffering, and loss. It tells us that we should learn as much as we can from any hardship we face, rather than resign ourselves to be victims to life's circumstances.
This applies to a wide variety of situations big or small."

Peter Andrews

Honor All Trees, All People

Apple, banyan, baobob, bodhi, cedar, cherry
blossom, chesnut, coconut, cottonwood,
cypress, elm, evergreen, fig, ginko, maple,
magnolia, mulberry, oak, olive, palm, pear,
pine, redwood, sequoia, spruce, and sycamore.
All are names of trees.

Some trees feed us, others inspire, nurture, or
shade us! Many trees are tied to our myths
and cultures.

Most of all trees, like people with all of their
beauty and differences are a unique reflection
of the Creator's magnificent wisdom to offer
joy; to share and provide for the physical and
spiritual needs of humanity.

In honoring all trees; honoring all people . . .

We learn to Honor the Creator!

Honor All Trees, All People

"Sometimes, I get emotional when I look at trees. No matter what the season, to me, a tree has year round beauty. When it comes to nature, they are my favorite.

Trees are so very expressive. In the summer they are fully dressed but no two are alike; much like human beings each has its own needs, style, shape and form.

Trees are very protective of the creatures living among the dressings of leaves.

Later the trees lose their leaves, and although they are naked for a while, their roots nourish them back. This cycle means for us not to give up hope because we have a nurturing Creator who cares for all creatures of the earth."

Gloria Brown

Occupation: Educator, Pittsburgh, PA **Spiritual Path:** Compassion, patience and understanding of others. **Dream for the World:** As Marvin Gaye sang—**"Let's Save the Children!"**

There Is No Me Without You!

One day a majestic butterfly came upon a dying caterpillar in a cocoon.

Re-membering her own metamorphosis she greeted him joyfully and said "Look at me! Don't be afraid. Now I know, there is no me without you!"

But the caterpillar didn't understand. He cried because he thought only of all he was losing and didn't yet know the majesty of who he was about to become!

Sometime we too must let go and allow Divine Majesty into our lives.

"There is no me without you!" said the majestic butterfly as she continued on her journey of love!

There Is No Me Without You!

"Of the many exquisite passages you have sent daily, none has spoken to me quite like the soon-to-transform caterpillar addressing the melancholy butterfly.

When I first started teaching in the fall of 1992, one of the first books to which my mentor in Baton Rouge, LA introduced me was Eric Carle's The Very Hungry Caterpillar.

I can still recall the artistry implicit in each illustration and seeming symphony of colors and textures imbued within the story. Nearly twenty years later, again and again I continue to cross paths with this timeless children's book in libraries, classrooms, book stores and workshops. Reading your dialogue as written on April 23, 2011, was a gorgeous reminder that conversation between the **present (caterpillar)** and **future (butterfly)** can often be the difference between **being mired in the past and reaching with both hands toward our future, unknown though it may be.**"

Tehuti Carter Jones

Occupation: Educator/Writer, United States of America **Dream for the World:** My dream for the world is that as humans we get out of its way and allow the world to reach its promise, that being optimal beauty.

There Is No Me Without You!

I chose this reflection of yours, found after we spoke on the phone . . . One of my favorites. It was a typical morning. I was ready to go to work on an account in Monmouth Beach, NJ area. I was driving along a beautiful coastal beach, when out of nowhere this intense, overwhelming vision came to me of angels!

There were two of them, one hovering above the other. One was looking ahead, hand held over the sibling's, the other look back.

Since this dramatic transmission has come and gone, other visions have passed through my hands onto canvas. My life has been enriched with blessings to help others.

Karen Piazza, Artist

A New Day

On an early morning not long ago it seemed the Sky was painted with whisperings of orange, and red and yellow, and green and purple. Grey white Clouds with tints of powder blue formed a pathway as the Moon began her journey back into the Universe. As she traveled the Compassionate Moon came upon the Sun who greeted her with a gentle kiss filled with understanding and love. Thus with the joining of Mother Moon and Father Sun came the Breath of Divine Grace and the Morning Star was born. Far away on planet Earth=Heart trees rustled in the wind with loving appreciation and respect for the dawn of a New Day. And throughout the world people of all cultures, religions and traditions rose in celebration and gave thanks for the Miracle of a New Day.

"There are so many of your words and meditations that reach deep inside me. This one is memorable in its appreciation and attention to our beautiful natural world, but also to the many paths we explore toward understanding (the best way we can) the mysteries and the miracles. And when you wrote this, baby Orion was only a week old (born on December 1) and that new dawn shone its morning light on this brand-new-to-the world boy.

Love is beautiful. And, as Orion's mama says, deep love can be shared in the families & friends we choose as well as the families into which we are born."

Andrea Christofferson

An Uncertain Path

Starting alone on an uncertain path.

In media res. Beginning in the middle.

Coming to light when least expected.

Nourished by the melting pot.

Things are how they should be.

The happiness in-between the moments of doubt.

Limping backwards, leaping ahead.

Seeking comfort in the curved spoon moon.

Bending upwards for vitality.

The tango between you and you.

Starting together on an uncertain path.

Adrienne Croix

Mother . . . . .

Maybe
Only
The
Heart = Earth
Explains
Reason . . . . .

For LOVE.

Seventy-Five Years of Gracious Living

A Dedication to Adele S. Dendy, Ed.D

Coming to Life
Surrounded by care and thoughtful prayers—
An "Angel" comes into being human
with resilient spirit intact.

A Modern Miracle
Spreads her wings blessing people—All as One.

Honoring our Creator
She spends precious time, molding while still healing her
children of un-duplicable, un-predictable life experiences—
Dreams, and Exposures.

Gracious and Grateful—
Her Wings of change offer trajectories of everlasting peace and love.

We exist humbled by her dedication—and selfless actions
over so many blessed years.

Coming to Life, surrounded by care and thoughtful prayers—
Our "Angel" is a human being with resilient spirit intact.

We are most thankful for the Angel of Life—Our Mother.

Forever Yours,

Kay Suszanna Dendy

Occupation: Business Development/Healing the people of
the world through manifestations of Personal and
Professional Goals **Spiritual Path**: The Creator Rules!
Dream for the World: That Humanity and all World Nature
Co-exist as One in the name of Love, Peace and Harmony!

31

Our Grand Children
By Gayle Hodnett Dobbs
For My Husband, Chuckie Dobbs

Painting a picture, or playing in the sand with your grandchildren is like falling in love all over again. Granma's hands, Pop Pop's joy. When you live long enough, one has the joy of grandchildren more precious than your own life!

My 40th Wedding Anniversary Musings

Love is . . . Being able to do all the silly things you wanted to do as a child, as you did with your children—you share with your grandchildren.

"Oh! The Places You Could Go" said Dr. Seuss . . . Disney World!!! It was the best vacation Pop Pop, my grandkids and I ever had! Until this year, when we took Naima and Kyree with us to Hawaii for a visit with the three younger grands—Che Pax, Plum and Rocket. I made waffles for all five grandchildren, one set of parents and the grandparents. Watching everyone eat the waffles—Priceless! That was love in action!

Back in Atlanta—talking to or seeing a grandchild at least once a week puts a smile on our face and a song in our heart bringing out the sun on any rainy day.

Love is . . . Watching and helping as our grandkids grow and learn! **Love is** . . . Seeing ourselves in our children and their children . . . . and knowing somehow, as my husband says . . . **"Everything Is Gonna Be Alright!"** *My hope and prayer for the world is peace from war and the elimination of hunger. God Bless Us, Every One!*

An Imprint of Love

Beloveds, All that you are, or hope to be lies within the imprint of love within your heart.

Love meets you and speaks to you through your heart.

Listen, and care fully.

Know always that you are loved and cherished by a Divine Presence. Love and cherish all before you.

Begin this day with a smile of love, and your every smile will become a prayerful love song throughout the Uni-Verse!"

"A Smile of Love for the Vampires of Dialysis"
By Reverend Sedrick Gardner

There is a new vampire; I'm not talking about Dark Shadow or an Ann Rice book. They have names like Davita, Fresenius, and Renal Advantage Inc.(R.A.I), but they are vampires nevertheless. They are dialysis clinics and I have willingly given my blood three times a week for the past three years. They say that they are cleansing my blood and returning it to me, but I always see the remnants of my blood in the tubing that they discard at the end of the process even though the tubing was clear in the beginning. **Yet I smile and give my blood willingly in love.**

At my last clinic they changed all the chairs into beds because they were going "nocturnal". I always heard that vampires preferred the dark. So I left that clinic which was owned by Fresnenius to go to a brand new clinic with a new name (R.A.I.) only to find out that all of the dialysis machines at the new clinic were made by Fresenius. **But I still smile in love**.

I learned a long time ago that in order to get beyond something that you no longer want in your life you cannot create an antagonistic relationship with the thing. That type of duality only creates a forever ongoing back and forth.

There is a way that you can love yourself out of a situation. So I smile and love the process.

"A Smile of Love for the Vampires of Dialysis" Cont

I love my technician Sharon who sticks me with two big needles (they don't use enlarged teeth anymore) each time I come for treatment. I see her as my little sister and we share life stories and good places to eat (There is something about dialysis that makes you ravenously hungry.)

I love my nurse Cynthia who uses the stethoscope to check my breathing before and after treatment. She was also my mother's dialysis nurse so I feel a certain kinship with her . . . Especially now that my mother has made her transition from this earth plane. **I love her and I know she loves me so I'd let her suck my blood anytime.**

I love my head nurse Sarah who seems to really be knowledgeable about dialysis practices and procedures and turns off the lights so we vampires can sleep.

I love the tech Leon because he is cool and has flowing locks to his butt . . . maybe even longer. My nickname for him is chocolate gum drop. I love the tech Richard who is a hard worker and you can tell by the sweat of his brow. I even love the tech Chris who doesn't even come to my side of the room much and rarely speaks to me. He is a young black male working and going to school to be a nurse so you have to love that. Afterall he could be doing so many other things that I dont love.

I love the clinic Director Lisa who self-proclaims herself as Queen Bee; even though I really never liked the Queen Bee type. But I love her because my life is in her hands and I have to trust that she will always do right by me. I love the social worker who helped me to get a supplement to my Medicare insurance; even though she told me that her company was saying it cost too much and they may stop paying for it. I found out the same day that Fresenius has bought R.A.I and when I look at their stock they are doing very well. I am sure that between she and I, we can create a miracle and they will pay the premium because we are both deeply spiritual people. **So I smile in love.**

"A Smile of Love
for the Vampires of Dialysis" Cont

I love my nutritionist that helped me to get the Renvela that they say I have to take each time I have a meal to keep my phophorous down; even though she let it run out, but yesterday she gave me the forms that allow me to re-order it myself and for that I love her with a smile.

And last but not least I love my doctor who is brilliant, and hardworking, and listens to my opinion and who gives compassionate loving advice. I will love these blood sucking vampires until I lift myself into a kidney transplant and then I will learn to love taking anti-rejection drugs every day for the rest of my life. I will love that with a smile too.

Rev. Sedrick Gardner

Spiritual Path: I acknowledge all major religions and am a minister at an interdenominational new thought church, Hillside International Truth Center in Atlanta, Georgia. **My dream for the world is enlightened peace and love for all mankind.**

Share your Gifts

Do not underestimate the power to positively affect the lives of others. We each are given gifts that can bring knowledge, and joy to others. Do not guard your gifts and sparingly share your knowledge with only those you know. Instead, share your gifts with all who welcome your intentions.

Sunil B. Gupta

Occupation: Lifelong student, **Spiritual Path:** Buddhism
Dream for the World: Clarity of vision

Beautiful Beacon

Oh Dear Melony,

Thank you with immense gratitude for your lovingkindness!

Please know how tremendously I cherish your friendship, love, light, and inspiration!

You are truly a beautiful beacon of luminous inspiration to us all, and you always magnanimously share your prodigious wisdom and exquisite, awe-inspiring heart and soul! :)

I am ardently anticipating reading your new book and know that it will be consciousness-expanding, powerful and transformative . . .

Sending infinite love and blessings to you always!

Katherine Henry

JOY

Joy is knowing GOD.

Joy is "La Madrugada," where night and
morning release their embrace and give way
to DAY.

Joy is in the birds that gently sing the
stars to sleep, and rouse the babies to
play. Joy is in Loving and
Caring and knowing. Joy is in you and me.

This reflection is based on "JOY', something that I seek for
myself and all of humanity. I live in the great metropolis
called New York City. I have four children and am a
Children's Librarian.

Patricia Moore

The Essence of Our Life
By Norbu Tsering

Being born naked but not shivering in the land of snow in Tibet, I used to hear the story of torture and demolishing the Tibetan monasteries and temples by the then Peoples Liberation Army of China. I saw many monasteries and temples being razed to the ground. I spent my early childhood as a shepherd, wide less grassland as my empire and sheep and goats as my subjects. Out of fear of persecution and lack of educational rights, my lone mother had made one of her greatest decision of sending me to India for education.

Living without one's parents since from 12 years of age was never easy and it's hard to imagine. But, then being admitted to the School of Orphans and those destitute at the vicinity of His Holiness the Dalai Lama, in India was a real blessing and opportunity.

After successfully finishing my school and graduation, I joined for the community service of Tibetan Government in exile as its civil servant. I was privileged to serve our community as accountant, Manager and Settlement Officer.

Life of more than two decades as a political refugee is painful and embarrassing. I was often harassed and victimized by the local authorities on any excuse in both India and Nepal.

Throughout my life, I came across my wonderful persons, whose help, directions and feelings had have been turning points of my life. Taking this opportunity, I cannot miss the name of Miss Melony. A wonderful lady, whose love, kindness and sense of sharing, I never doubted.

The Essence of Our Life Cont

Above all, one of the best things that I have experienced throughout my life and one of the best things that I have been deeply taught by my religion is Love and kindness.

Giving love and showing kindness for others is the most satisfying things and the best asset that one could have when one leaves from this world.

Besides, I truly believe that there always is best thing to happen at the particular movement no matter how difficult and long it may take. It happens for better and if it doesn't happen, it happens on another time with a better prospect. God is great and He is the greatest.

With prayers and love for all of sentient beings,

Norbu Tsering

LOVE

"Many Waters Cannot Quench Love, Neither Can The Floods Drown It" Song Of Solomon 8:7

It is my belief that love is the most powerful force in the universe and represents the greatest hope for permanence and stability. As an artist, it has not only sustained me, but has been the catalyst and raison d' etre for why I create, move and have my being. **Purposeful work is work rooted in love.**

When we begin to understand love as a direct source of life and light, we tap into an inexhaustible spring of the Living God and our Sacred Humanity. It is in this place that we truly flourish, challenge our comfort zones and embrace the unknown without fear or trepidation.

Holy Scriptures remind us that **"Perfect Love Casts Out All Fear"**. When we embrace the transformational qualities of love, the higher self is exalted. We in fact begin to live more authentically, transparently and joyfully in the center of truth.

If all the world could dance as one, all the possibilities of universal unity could be realized!

Reginald Yates

Occupation: Artist   **Spiritual Path:** Christian

The Healing Adagio . . .

Part Three

Daily Reminders for

Living the Song

and

Doing the Dance

Always Believe

If you do not believe
that you have the potential
to achieve your desires,
then you will not achieve them.

Within you is the gift
of unlimited potential.

Discover it!
Develop, use and share
your unique gifts
to achieve your good desires.

Believe in the unlimited power of you!

Always Love You

Do You Love You?
So often our negative actions towards others reflect
some deep pain or woundedness within ourselves.

Today nurture yourself, forgive and love all of you!
G-d loves you, all of you!

**Always love you, because when you love
yourself, you have more love to share!**

Assigning Blame

When someone offers you their trust
and seeks your counsel,
regarding a difficult situation,
try not to say
"I think it was your fault".

They may have been honestly seeking understanding.

They may have come to you
looking for support so they
could be a better person.

**Once we assign blame,
communications often break down
and it becomes harder to
create a win, win resolution.**

Today, try to truly listen with compassion.

**Be a Builder of Bridges,
Not a Breaker of Hearts!**

Awaken In Gratitude

Every day we awaken in gratitude, every time we say thank you, every step we take with appreciation allows us to share our hope. Hope guides us in preparation and allows us to clear our minds, our hearts and our homes so that we have space to grow. When we let go of our attachment to that which no longer serves us, we make room for all the good that is coming!

Balance & Beauty

When we are feeling the weight of the world with all our frailties and imperfections; we have only to re-member Love. Love gives us the glimmering moon, stars and planets so that we may imagine the vastness of the Uni-Verse and experience light even in darkness. And then, so that we may honor our Mother Earth-Heart, and all her creations, we are given the kiss of the rising Sun to nurture us with hope and re-birth each new day. This is the balance and beauty of Love!

Beautiful

Beautiful is the one who overcomes fear; forsakes greed; understands pain; shares the gifts of their heart; and moves forward joyfully into the light of love to meet their destiny! Each of You are Beautiful Spirits ever-awakening and moving forward in Grace! **You Are Beautiful!**

Becoming

Your journey, no matter how difficult will create the jewels of wisdom in your heart. Have mercy and compassion for yourself and others so that you grow in understanding. Look beyond the discord. Be tolerant and kind. Then you . . . All that you will Become is—**Magnificent in Timeless Love**.

Being Flexible

Life will call on us to be flexible. Our attachment to every immediate outcome can limit Grace. When we are patient with ourselves and others, we learn that a change in plans often means the time is not right or that w e will receive an unexpected, unanticipated gift of a lesson in love. No matter your disappointment, be gracious and flexible. Embrace the change, honor the Grace, the Dance and Song of Universe. Joyfully live the miracle that is your life!

Being Present

When those around you appear grouchy and irritable, offer your compassion. Give them a little space. Be patient. Try not to take it as an attack on you. Remember that there may be something big troubling them in their lives. They need your prayers and good thoughts; **not your condemnation.** Your care and gentleness is a gift. Always try to be Present with Love!

Being Strategic

Life often calls for us to be strategic.

There are many paths

but all lead back to the compassionate heart.

Today be strategic,

embrace your forgotten understanding.

Open up to divine wisdom and grace.

Take time to live this moment

with profound humility.

When you take a wrong turn,

stop,

breathe;

and with your heart open—

Be Strategic.

Re-think your route.

Being Wise

In life we may be asked to be-friend
both a fool and a wise one.

The fool will smile and charm us,
take our gifts, ask for more, break their word,
and soon leave to find others to manipulate.

Be always kind.

A wise one asks for nothing, shares
whatever they have
and vows eternal friendship.

Be grateful to the fool
for they have served as a teacher
and you have learned who NOT to become.

Pray for them.

To the wise one, offer friendship,
pray together and begin to build
a universal community of good
with a loving foundation.

Are you a fool or a wise one?

Bold Heart

When we pay attention

to the details of life

and listen to all that is said

or not said . . .

We develop clarity

and a knowingness of truth.

Truth commands

that we develop our own self—discipline.

Then we are able to move forward

with a clear vision

and a bold heart!

What is you truth?

How will you move forward?

Today, listen carefully.

Embrace your vision.

Have a Bold Heart. Enjoy Your Journey!

Build New Bridges

Beloveds, why do we disdain each other?

Your blood is as red as my blood and our tears both taste salty, like the ocean.

You have mourned your lost dreams and loved ones, as I have mourned mine.

As I watch our children happily playing together, new dreams emerge and to you I offer my hand in friendship.

We cannot change our yesterdays.

What we can do is to begin this new day in appreciation of our children as our most precious gifts.

Our children offer love and dream of building bridges of understanding and joy. This dream for is possible only through our compassionate hearts.

Affirmation

Today let us honor the dreams of our children. We will use the tools of our hearts—compassion, hope, forgiveness, kindness, patience, sharing and understanding. **Together we build new bridges of joy and hope for a better world for our children. This is love in action—love infinite in divine possibility!**

Calling All Dreamers

We must be grateful for our dreamers. It is our collective dream of peace and our commitment to goodness moment to moment that allows us to be kind in a world that has lost its moral compass. Today, the Uni-Verse is calling all dreamers! Live inspired. Offer and Be your best in goodness. Sing of hope. Embrace, believe and live the collective dream!

Choosing Empathy

We learn something important about ourselves when we pay attention to how we respond to others in need. Every time we choose to offer empathy and compassion, a new flower of love blossoms in the universal garden of hope!

Comfort Zone

Perhaps there will come a time in your life when you are given a situation where you must step out of comfort zone to achieve that which you most desire. Have courage. Breathe deeply. Gather your energy and strength. Believe that you can. No obstacle is too big. Believe that there is unseen support. **Take the next step into your good destiny!**

Love Awaits!

Compromise

We may look and think differently.
We may live in different climates
and sing different songs.

Still we all are born from the Heart of Love.

When we learn to honor
and respect our differences,
we can come together to make our lives better.
In difference we must learn to share and compromise!

Core Values

In order to know peace,
we must remain rooted in our core values;
in the traditions that enrich us;
and in the constant nurturing of kindness.
We must never let technology dictate
or replace compassionate common sense
and our willingness to honor
our core values of faith, hope, mercy and charity.

Deception

When you walk with an open heart,
there are those who will try
to deceive you.

They may even believe that
your kindness is a weakness.

They may lie and try to steal
your money and your heart.

This is a fact of life.

When you know this,
you become wealthy
in understanding and wisdom.

You become stronger
in love and compassion.

No matter what others believe,
you see every deception.

But as an instrument of God,
you pray for the best.

You Give with discernment;
lovingly.

And your gifts forever
multiply with love!

This is the reward
for the believer
and giver of love!

Dis-Agreement

We have all had our disagreements.

Still we must always find a way

to be the peace,

and make the peace.

Knowing this, today in disagreement,

have this thought . . . .

"I will take steps towards you

in integrity and loving grace.

My hope is that you will meet me halfway.

Still if you are unable

to make the journey,

I will understand and

keep walking until

we are side by side.

Then I will offer my hand in hope,

and respect with compassion."

Today, Make the Peace,
Be the PEACE!!!

Don't Forget

There may be no tomorrow

but we do have today.

Embrace this moment,

in this time and place.

With love, allow your heart

to open and make some new space.

Smile at stranger.

Call an old friend.

Don't forget in life

we must all learn to bend.

Today live like you dreamed you would . . . .

Love like you know you should!

Encouragement

When we offer our encouragement to others and nurture their good ideas as we nurture our own, the garden becomes a beautiful community. Encouraging each other, dreaming and working together for good bears fruit that feeds and nurtures the Divine Spirit in All! **Today, be a light of Encouragement!**

First, Show Up!

We often think we have a good reason to second guess our hearts but the beauty in life comes when we choose to show up, and be fully present in the moment. Today honor yourself, offer your best and enjoy the beautiful fruit that Our Creator has planned for you. The Uni-verse is singing—this is your life. Offer your best! **You must show up and be present to receive your blessings!**

Follow the Light

A Seeker of Truth will learn to let go of anger and try each day to embrace forgiveness by offering gifts of compassion to all those in need of love. Some will call you a fool. Others will feel that you have betrayed them. Forgive them, for they do not yet understand the power of a healing heart. The more you share the Best of You, the brighter the light of love. Follow the Light and you, yourself will light the way for others when they are ready!!

Friends

A true friend doesn't care what your title is or how much money you have in the bank. A true friend is an Earth Angel that helps you get back on your path when you didn't even know you were lost!

Fruit for Life

Moment to moment throughout eternity, the fruit will always be bountiful when we have faith in Good. Each of us will have the opportunity to be a witness, a giver, a receiver, and a believer of love! Visit the garden of your heart; and you will savor and enjoy fruit for life!

Gift of Circumstance

May you feel
the infinite power of love
and walk with divine grace
through the sunshine and rain,
in darkness and in light;
as you move through each life challenge.

May you come to understand that in every circumstance
lays a new gift of the universe waiting to be discovered.

May your love be magnified
as you express your genuine gratitude
for living this,
and every moment!

**Today please remember that there
is infinite power in abiding love!**

Gifts of Your Heart

A smile, or a hug can be precious
if it is given from the heart.

A note written to say "how are you?"
"Happy birthday!" or "I love you!"
may be cherished for a lifetime . . .

A phone call to an old friend
letting them know that you are
thinking of them may bring tears to their eyes.

A visit to a sick friend,
just sitting quietly holding their hand
can let them know they are loved
and make a difficult time easier to bear.

These are the gifts of the heart
that may be filled with infinite love.

Be a loving tool of divine grace.

Always try to offer encouragement to others.

No matter the occasion or just because,

share the many gifts of your heart!

Good Wishes

Prayer and good wishes coupled with courage and unselfish acts of kindness create hope in the hearts of many and allow faith to light the path on a difficult journey!

Today I pray that the spirit of goodness will share courage and undaunted faith so that we offer unselfish acts of kindness and bring hope to many!

Healing Oasis

No matter what others tell us the odds are,

when we have courage

to embrace a difficult day

and say "I am ready",

then peace will be the calling

and answer of your heart.

Peace is a vibration

filled with dignity and loving intent.

Peace empowers you with faith

and gives you the hope

and strength you need

to journey to the Healing Oasis.

Honor the Song of Life

When we think of life as a song, we are able to the live the melody.

Life as a song also requires that we come together and sing our many different parts.

Whether you are an alto, a soprano, a tenor, a baritone or bass, we can all learn to sing and live in harmony when we embrace and honor the exquisite melody of the Song of Life!

Impatience

In today's world,
we often expect others to offer
us kindness even when we are impatient.
We say "It's their job.
Can't they move faster?".

Yet sometimes in our hurriedness
and disregard, we forget
to show our gratitude—
to say please and thank you
or to see others as worthy
of our civility.

Today, please try to show your civility.

Be patient—look into someone's eyes,
smile and express your appreciation
for even the smallest deed.

It may bring you both a moment of joy!

In Difficulty

Many in great difficulty have heard the re-assuring voice that says, *"I will walk with you throughout life. Sometimes it will appear that I am behind you. Other times that I am ahead or beside you. When you fall I will pick you up. Have faith and believe. Like a phoenix, we will fly with hope and share Our Love."* **When we listen to the VOICE, we embrace peace and understand that the Infinite Power of Love resides within each of us! We Are Never Alone!**

Journey of the Butterfly

After having flown together in glory, **Mama and Papa Butterflies hibernate**. Spring marks the time when they come together in love, mate and create the next generation called **Caterpillars**. Then slipping into the breath of eternity, off to Heaven the Butterflies go. The new Caterpillars eat and grow. As they become wiser, they shed layers of skin and embracing the unknown, become a **Chrysalis shell**. Nurturing themselves within the protection their Chrysalis, they soon grow and become the new beautiful, exquisite Mama and Papa Butterflies. **This is the Metamorphosis of Life.**

Like Yourself, Laugh Often

Today like yourself, laugh often and live life with faith. Be still for a moment. Breathe deeply, again and again. Now receive—and embrace the ever encompassing wisdom of divine spirit. Have courage. In your head dance with hope, sing of love. Yes it is okay to be marvelous! Now go and share the wealth of your ever loving heart.

Limitedless Riches

Our riches are limitedless.

We have the potential to feed all those hungry on this earth.

And if wealth was the warmth, the love and giving spirit of our

hearts, we would all be billionaires.

In fact, G-d believes we are!

Today, re-discover the joy and love within you.

You are a billionaire and have much to share with the world!

Now open your heart with infinite love.

Begin to feed those who are hurting,

disillusioned and in need of love!

Remind them, as you have been reminded—

in G-d's heart we each have a special,

unique gift to share.

We Are All Billionaires!

Listening

Let us begin this day in faith;
knowing that any obstacle
is a part of our journey in grace.

Meet each being in love.

Offer your hand
with compassion and respect.

Listen in appreciation
to their unique perspective.

Living Good Answers

We all make mistakes.

Then hopefully we search for a solution,
not in anger but in love.

Often when we are angry,
no one can help us
because we are not honest
in our questions to ourselves.

Therefore we cannot learn to live good answers.

Affirmation

Today I will question and be honest with myself.
I will see myself in all beings and offer only my best in love.
Honesty, understanding and compassion are tools that help me
to live good answers!

Love As Innocence

If we are to honor the core of our faith traditions
then we ourselves must say **No More War**!

We must put down our weapons,
let go of our fear, look beyond judgment,
offer compassion and forgiveness
to "our enemies" and return
to the innocence of the loving heart.

When we begin to see all beings
as gifts of the Blessed Creator,
we recognize that they too desire what we desire.

We all desire,
thrive and blossom in the
innocence and hope of Love!

Love, the Foundation

As I look at a bed of flowers or a tree seeped in the brown colored dirt of my skin, I think also of dolphins and fish swimming in the blue green ocean. I am in awe!

I taste a banana, an apple, an avocado or any fruit or vegetable of our earth and I feel in it the sun that nourishes us. And on a clear night I stare in wonderment at faraway clouds and stars that appear to dance with the moon.

I breathe deeply and think—"surely within our hearts is the memory of a Divine Creator passionately in love with us all!"
And as always, then I return to love as the foundation of my life.

MERCY

Children often teach us mercy.
A child will feel your hurt
and offer you a hand
or a hug and say "I love you!".

Children believe that
to share their love
heals hurt and pain.

Like children, we too can
offer mercy and extend a hand
in lovingly compassion.

We too should be willing
to offer the gentle gifts of our heart!

Moving East

When most people are moving west
but your heart says go east,
have the courage to follow your heart!

You will learn new lessons from all sentient beings.

The rocks and trees will guide you.

Flowers and other vegetation will nourish you.

Birds and the wind will teach you songs of Grace.

The sun, the moon and the stars will provide loving solace.

Have faith in love.

Go East with divine blessings of strength.

Climb your personal mountains.

Rest in the valleys.

Hear the echo of Hope.

Live Your Destiny!

New Doors

Life will ask us to let go and move on!

Sometimes it is difficult but what awaits us in love
is better than our minds or egos can anticipate.

Every step we take is special.

Cherish the moment.
Hone your skills of caring and compassion.
Prepare to move on with your soul's purpose.

Keep your heart open.
Follow the Divine Path of Forgiveness.

Love, hard work and patience will open New Doors of Grace!

Nurture a Friendship

A friend is there on the sunny days
and through the storms of life.

Time may have sent you both
in different directions as life moved on.

Still friendship is a precious gift
that remains always in our hearts.

It is good to cherish our friends,
and nurture our friendships
through all the seasons of our lives!

People

People are different and All are special!

People come in different sizes, shapes
and have different colored eyes,
and hair and skin!

People live in different countries where there
are different cultures and traditions on mostly
five continents even though there are seven
continents on Earth.

People speak many different languages too!
They may play different instruments and sing
different songs.

People are different but there is one song
everybody can learn to sing and harmonize
together.

We call it the Song of Love!

Please Be Yourself!

The next time we meet along the way, promise me this . . .
Please, just be yourself.

Write your own song.
Do your own dance.

Allow me the gift of discovering and accepting the mystery of You!

Within that mystery, Grace will move.
Then with ease, I will sing and dance too! Please just Be You!

Remember, I only know how to Be Me!

Prepare for Dissonance

When you are doing good in the world,

there will be voices of dissonance.

People will tell you it's not possible

to do better and that you should be satisfied

with the way it is.

They may try hard to fill you with their own fearful thoughts.

Prepare for Dissonance.

You can choose not to embrace their fear!

Each day is a new day filled with hope and courage.

Listen to the divine whispers of your heart.

Be who you are.

Use your gifts for good.

Do your work.

Today, keep doing good

and allow love always to abide in you!

Picture of Love

Each day we have the opportunity

to create a picture of love for eternity!

Today be kind to all.

Preserve and paint every heart

with precious, positive memories!

Today—be joyful. Live, and love!

Releasing Obligation

When we are able to let go and release others

of their feelings of obligation or guilt towards us,

then love in its freedom begins to permeate

the sweet scent and memory of Divine Understanding!

The flames of that love never die but are transformed.

The heat of love's intensity creates a jewel for healing.

Throughout every lifetime, as the embers simmer

and glow within the heart,

that love re-membered . . . .

becomes

an emerald permeating the sweet scent

and memory of Divine Understanding!

Romance

For all the times I've loved
and all the people I've loved
it's never been the same.

I am in love with children,
butterflies, birds, flowers, trees,
stones, seashells and dolphins.

I love people who love
and people trying to love.

I love the sun, the rain,
the moon and the stars!

I even love people who have forgotten how to love
because they teach me to keep my heart open.

I love Being Alive . . . And See Life As An Everlasting Spiritual Romance!

Sparkling Bright Light

Many have said that this is a time of great darkness. It could be, because some have lost value for the divine beauty and simplicity of life. Still within the darkness—by our questioning and our search for light, we can come to a new understanding. When we embrace love without fear as our practice, we heal.—In our healing, we become sparkling, bright lights within the universe. The truth is, all things grow and heal with love and become infused with divine light. **Today sparkle with your loving actions and feel your blessings and gifts multiply! Shine on!**

Spontaneous Gifts

If I have learned anything, it is that I am humbled most by the spontaneous gifts of those facing major life challenges and those who have little—but willing share their smiles, appreciation, kind words and big hearts with loving joy. Their many gifts inspire me to be a better person, to want to be of greater service, to keep my word and to reflect the joy, respect and appreciation for people, and life on this planet that others have so openly shared with me!

Surrender

When we are at war in our heart, we try to protect ourselves from being hurt, and create a fortress of quiet despair. We carry old wounds like badges of honor and are often ready to battle. When we surrender in love and believe in good, we are asking for divine guidance and support. We re-member to trust that every experience offers a lesson in understanding. We then open the door to forgiveness and experience cherished new gifts that we had not anticipated but arrive in that glorious moment! **Surrender and Live Well With LOVE!**

Tenacity

If we are to accomplish our goal
of climbing the mountain,
then we need to acquire tenacity
to fuel our passion
with constant good efforts
as we walk;
and remember to rest when needed!

Transformative Chaos

We cannot help but feel uncomfortable in this world of transformative chaos!

Greed and War can no longer financially or emotionally sustain us. Only cooperative collective acts of compassion and love can do that.

Current chaos represents our dreams of a vivid and lasting peace. Change will come whether or not we are ready.

Set your clear loving intention with hope.

Have faith.

Throughout this chaotic transformation we must rest more;

be truthful and judicious in our thoughts and actions;

offer forgiveness with mercy, and **move forward in love**.

When the Glass Has Broken

Have you ever broken a favorite glass and felt dismayed
at its shattering?

For many of us, our lives have been shattered in
disappointment by economic disparity, lost hope and
grief from war.

Just as we step gingerly and pick up the pieces of
glass to be discarded, so we must honor our grief and
dis-appointment in ritual.

Then let it go with forgiveness so that envy, greed and
violence do not become the broken glass of your heart.

Begin today by tenderly
nurturing yourself and others.

Re-capture in gratitude, the hopes and
dreams of your resilience, appreciating,
peaceful, sharing, loving heart.

The Healing Adagio . . .

Part Four
Re-membering
Wisdom

Re-Discovering
Hope

Hearts Stand

When you listen to the dolphins laugh
and hear the roar of whales;
or awaken to the gentle call
of birds singing in hope
or embrace the scents of trees and flowers;
and humbly honor All that has been
divinely created on Earth
with your thank yous . . . .

Then you will know that
the heart alone stands
in the sands of time
through the Greatness of Love.

How will you live the Answer?

All that I write has been said before. It has been written in
our sacred texts and lived by the gentle Masters who have
come to guide us.
It is We, as a Collective that must learn to take heed.
In the world today, we are focusing our resources and
attention on sustaining the desires and materialist greed of
the corrupt.

Too many billions of us are living in poverty without
adequate shelter, education or healthcare.
Too many of us are becoming drunk
with idea of materialist success
and we listen to those
who incite fear and divide us.

Only love will heal and unite us.

We are many people, many cultures, many religions. We must
learn to respect eachother, and to support those in need. Our
willingness to love one another and to want for others what we
want for ourselves is the most important mandate of the world
today.
Will we learn to share and live together in peace
with respect and love? This is the question.

How will you live the answer?

Culture of WAR

This Culture of War masked in hopes of freedom
promotes the death of peaceful dreams and makes
victims and survivors, not victors!

For no matter what side wins—
the broken hearts, the missing arms or legs,
the sound of bombs, machine guns
and mortar mixed with the screams of
children, women, and men
replay over and over in the brain
years later . . .

As innocent children needing nurturing
offer us love and attention
which in our woundedness we ignore!

When will humanity learn that

compromise, cooperation, forgiveness, truth,

reconciliation

and Love for our-selves,

and our neighbors

is the only pathway of a good future?

Divine Intention

Each day some of us listen to commentators on the radio or
television who breed hate and incite fear.

Many of us don't know whom to trust.
Our media is creating insanity day after day.

Stop allowing voices of hate, fear and separation to control your
understanding.
Turn your tv, your talk radio and computer off!

Have good conversations with your children.
Read books to your children.
Sing songs and play games with your children.

Teach your children—so that you re-member
the divine life principles . . .

"Thou shalt not kill or steal.
Honor your mother, your father and all elders.
Love one another and honor your neighbor as yourself!"

Today, listen to the Divine within You.
Trust your heart.
Be discerning, kind,
and respectful to others—even when you disagree!

Begin to live, and love with Divine Intention!

The Destiny of Our Collective Gratitude

Spring is always a time for our re-birth and awakening.
It allows us to express our gratitude
and re-new our visions
of helping to heal our Mother Earth=Heart.

There are so many reasons to be grateful . . . .

But it also is a time for us to examine our hearts
and to pose a few questions.

Why do we squash our gratitude with greed?
Why do we make killing a necessary norm,
instead loving our neighbors as members
of our human and sentient family?

We are so often careless in the way we treat others,
and the way we treat our Mother Earth=Heart.

Our disregard is evident in the smallest things.

The piece of paper that one throws on to the ground
soon amounts to streets strew with garbage.

The unkind words we use when we simply disagree
become landmines and killing fields
that result in deep wounds of the heart.

This then leads to militaristic campaigns
where both soldiers and civilians
including mothers and children are killed recklessly
and without regard to our Collective ONENESS.

The Destiny of Our Collective Gratitude Cont

Is this the choice we really desire
to make in our hearts?
Our minds often appear to thrive
in the "Us versus THEM" paradigm.

Have we lost our way? What is our Collective Destiny?

It is interesting . . . for all those
who have awakened with fear
**many more are awakening with deep love
for all sentient beings.**

And as we awaken, we learn
to breathe deep soulful breaths—
and come to understand that
within the breath is the hope of Universal Spirit.

Each day more humans awaken with a tingling,
a new sense of humility and a desire
for new compassionate understanding.

One might say that we are like the buds
of cherry blossoms, magnolias,
or orchids in the Springtime.

How do YOU choose to blossom this Spring?

Will you allow your ego to fill you with new visions of fear
or will you embrace the nurturing breath of Divine Spirit.

**Chose Well Beloved . . . for your choice
helps determine our Collective Destiny of Gratitude.**

The Heart of G-d

Beloveds,
These are challenging times
and many across the universe are suffering.
Still, we must re-member that we are NEVER alone.

Yes, there are many moments and tunnels of despair. As we
learn from those living in Haiti, Gaza, Sudan, Tibet or from our
wise neighbor next door—faith will see us through.

And Yes, there are those of us still using violence
and destroying innocents while calling on G-d to fuel fear in the
heart of humanity.

Though some are walking in fear and resorting to violence, we
do have the continued opportunity to reflect the infinite peace
and mercy of G-d's heart.

How does this happen?
Perhaps it happens through our tears and the clearing of our
hearts.

When we release our fears and our anger,
we embrace an easiness
with a sense of relief and hope.

Just for a moment, embrace your fear
and then release it.

Sit with your new understanding
and feel your faith ignited into the light of love.

The Heart of G-d Cont

Divine Spirit is with us through each peril and
tribulation—asking us to see true value in the gift of life; to
honor and respect all others.

Today let us be filled with gratitude and truth.
**The truth is that there is more beauty in this world than
not.**

We are given the gift of understanding
and as we sit with this gift,
mercy and compassion pour through us.

And let us live this truth . . .
No matter our tradition, we are more the same than different let
us look to the root of life
and re-member our inter-connectedness.

We come from the **Heart of G-d** and always,
Divine Spirit is within us, encouraging us—asking us to forgive
ourselves and all others.

This Is The Word Of LOVE!

Re-Membering the Ancients: A Message from Our Eternal Grandmothers and Grandfathers

The sun shone on a crisp Fall day,
and the wind blew so that leaves
danced as old friends, and eternal lovers.
Even now the music plays in my head.
A drum beats steadily
as bells create joyful melodies of Grace.

It was then that many were reborn.
Reborn with the understanding
that love is patience in the knowing
and feeling of humility, and compassion.

Many were re-born knowing
love is all there is, and ever was.

And therefore it is no surprise
that today we find ourselves
amongst the fallen red/orange/yellow/green leaves
and gather them tenderly
as if they are our most precious possessions.

For these leaves represent
the passage of time—a settling,
an understanding,
an appreciation of Grace.

The Ancient Grandmothers and Grandfathers
are surprised,really,
that we don't re-member
to fully embrace the breath of our hearts.

Re-membering the Ancients: A Message from Our Eternal Grandmothers and Grandfathers–Cont

It is a breath as sweet as jasmine,
as salty as an ocean breeze,
as light and refreshing
as the smell of trees when it rains.
The breath is all things
that allow us a new understanding of the old.

We often have reason for celebration
for we are ancient in our desire,
in our faith, and our understanding.

And re-member, since the beginning of time
It has been said that
peace is a pathway that lies
beneath each thought, feeling, and action.

Peace is an opportunity
to create a world of tranquility
filled with hope, and manifested by healing.

Peace is the smile of joy
on a child's face as she or he
holds the hand of a grandparent
and adoringly they say to each other,
I love you!

Peace is each of us re-visiting our anger
and forgiving ourselves through love.

Peace is honoring the healing process
and holding a space for the joy
that can come after.

Peace is each of us walking tranquilly
with no guns, no weapons of mass destruction,
and no more red buttons in the white house
created to annihilate the world.
Re-membering the Ancients: A Message from Our Eternal
Grandmothers and Grandfathers-Cont

Peace is hope, day and night
illuminated by hard work, and the quest
for cures of all the ills of our society.

Peace is illuminated by each step into grace
and the reconciliation of differences
that now serve to plant
new seeds in our Universal Garden.

The Ancients are surprised, really,
that we don't re-member harmonics
as the flowers of Grace which eternally
have formed new bouquets of hope,
of infinite healing, of courage,
of solutions to age old challenges.

These bouquets honor and salute
our entire sentient family
and reflect a unique understanding
of the future of the Universe.

**The Ancients
are asking us to become
more aware of a special sense of order.**

Rebirth, transformations,
endings, beginnings again, and again
remind us that there is always cause for celebration,
always an opportunity to expand our vision,
and our hearts.

The Ancients are asking
Us to pay more attention;
to walk in the field of miracles,
to embrace the newness of leaves
fallen with hope, appreciation and courage.

Re-membering the Ancients: A Message from Our Eternal Grandmothers and Grandfathers–Cont

What if in this moment we imagine
a potential new healing
supported by angels, masters and spirit guides
as well as trees, mountains, oceans,
sea lions, eagles, doves, dolphins and whales.

The Ancients tell us that
truth is the constant re-minder
and the unearthing in the Now.
truth is the intuition and courage
within each of us.

Truth is the desire to live, hope and dream
of love—of a tranquil world with opportunity,
healing, food, equity,
and the fulfillment of good dreams for all.

Truth is a new song created by the symphony.

The chords are stronger, the harmony intensified.
Surety is the reality.
Resistance too is a part of the song.

**Together it all becomes a symphony of love
within the passage of time.**

Love traveling through unknown pathways.
Love with new purpose.
Love with new meaning.
It is a song where fear is transformed
into hope with the courage to take
a solo of compassion created by humility.

The symphony of love creates a
New Infinite Harmonic
that carries us beyond; in this time,
and beyond, the beyond, the beyond!

Re-membering the Ancients: A Message from Our Eternal Grandmothers and Grandfathers-Cont

The Ancients always remind us
that Joy is in the be-ing,
in the recognizing, in the acceptance of love.
As breathing creates the pathway
for the journey of love
into new sound vibrations of Harmonic Grace.

The Sun shone on a crisp Fall day,
and the wind blew so that leaves
danced as old friends, and eternal lovers.

And all the Ancient Grandmothers, and Grandfathers
are surprised; really,
that we don't re-member harmonics
as the flowers of Grace which eternally
have formed new bouquets of hope,
of infinite healing, of courage,
and solutions to age old challenges.

Now Please Re-member Harmonics

as the gift of love

that moves through YOU.

Tyrants last Stand

Let us thank each remarkable being that shares strength, courage, and joy or teaches us lessons that help us grow in love. May we live this day, and every day growing in awareness and walking as beings of compassionate appreciation and understanding. **There are many heroines and heroes among us!** Even as these times on Earth reveal a schism of selfishness, there is a mass awakening of sentient beings expressing their true loving selves. Miracles lay strewn in every path we walk, bringing us new gifts. Unfortunately this is a time of intense agony for those suffering in the mire of fear and dis-connected from Divine Spirit. **Tyrants around the world will continue to try to assert their ungodly will as they take their last stand.** Still everywhere we can feel the ecstasy of Earth Angels awakening and soaring with the Spirit of compassion and love. **Though many are experiencing the most dire of circumstances, our children will continue to act as beacons of light.** Nurture and pay attention to the children. They bring us hope and loving wonder. Through the innocence of our children, we are often inspired with new faith. **Honor our elders with unconditional love;** for they have shown us the way and held the space for our awakening. They too are important teachers. Every day, **small seeds of wisdom are given to us through our willingness to accept Divine Grace.** We have the opportunity us to grow in awareness, respect for eachother and love. Today please re-member that **love is a verb—an action word**. It can also be an adjective or a noun. As each one of us becomes love, we also become a heroine or hero. Together as we blossom, we will flourish and multiply in goodness.

And through goodness, Heaven On Earth will be restored. This is the word of LOVE!

Peacemaker 2001

You are a peacemaker mandated
to create a montage of LOVE all around the earth.
What will you do?

What if right now you are asked
to become a vessel of the Divine Heart . . .
Will you set aside your hidden fears?
Can you have the courage,
integrity and propensity to share your LOVE?

If you meet someone different than you,
suffering from xenophobia
and they are extremely unkind
because all they know is fear and hatred . . .
will you show them how to be
mellifluous with LOVE for ALL people?

You Have Awakened.
You are Re-Membering your dreams of LOVE.

Peacemaker 2001 Cont

Intrinsic in you is the desire

to create overtures of LOVE

for our children . . .

and all people through education, business, government,

art, music, dance, theatre and all art forms.

What Will You Do?

Every sentient being is an incarnation of LOVE.

LOVE is another name for

an Exalted Spirit with a palatial heart.

How Do You Feel?

Now, imagine yourself as a Lodestar

kindling the flame of LOVE.

Your best friend is Morning Star,

also known as Venus, the planet of LOVE.

You were born with the awareness of angels?

Together How Do You Feel And What Will You Do???

September 9, 2001

Peacemaker 2011

Peacemakers grow to see every side,
as they learn to read between, below,
and on top of words and emotions.

Peacemakers articulate a truth
that allows for compassion,
forgiveness and reconciliation.

They learn to walk and offer their lives
as living prayers for Cooperation and Peace.

Are you a Peacemaker?

How do you walk?
What truth will you articulate?

What Is Your Offering?

Success at the Oasis

Beloveds,

Even if it looks like
we will fail in our efforts for peace,
we must continue to believe that
our efforts have value.

Success lies in our willingness
to walk through
the desert of despair
and to keep sharing the love
in our hearts—no matter what!
We will reach the oasis!

True Power

Some of us have come to believe that control gives us power.
Some call others subordinates and think that their position of
wealth allows them privilege and respect.

This is mis-understanding.

Each human being is worthy of love and respect.
No human is less.

We all become greater when we honor those around us and
offer our resources to those in need with joy and appreciation
for their contributions. True power comes with integrity,
inspiration, and loving Grace.

The Black Crow

The caw-caw of the black crow singing of it's woe shares an important lesson we all need to know. He sings of greed and the old debt that has become every nation's biggest threat. The greedy want to jab, stab and grab. The caw-caw of the black crow sings to compromise, sow and grow. The lesson always is to care and share! Today Pray that people find the way! Pray that Good will save the day!

Open the Door!

In the still of the night; at dawn and throughout the day; into dusk and evening—always we are being asked to open the door for Love.

Love is ever-present in the whispers of the wind and even the harsh storms. Love calls to us with mercy and asks only that we acknowledge its fruitful presence in our lives.

So many are not listening.
Still the voice and song of Love travels throughout the ethers of time and offers hope to those who are willing.

Today is a day for simple miracles of hope and compassion. Awaken, open the door; and accept the fruit of Love!

Good Change and Healing

Good Change will come in the world only if we are diligent in our faith, let go of our greedy egos and begin to share our resources with hope and a desire to heal the many wounded hearts. Healing comes when we open our hearts with forgiveness and accept that we must collectively find a good way to feed every mind, body and spirit with cooperative caring and respect! Good Change and Healing begins with You!

Roots of Integrity

When it appears that there is no way to decide which way to go, stop and, breathe deeply over and over!

Look for the common ground in your choices. Examine the roots of integrity that rest in your heart.

What can be of benefit to peace? How can your actions contribute to good?

Now Begin Again. Have confidence in your decision.

With Integrity, You Step Into Grace!

Trust

Sometimes there will be no immediate evidence that your life
has moved in the right direction.
Things may appear to be the same, or even worse.
This is when we must trust and love.

Often the fruits of our good efforts are hidden in the clouds and
will come after the storms have subsided.

Keep nurturing good; love, trust and believe that the fruits of
your labor will come after the storms!

Be an Instrument of Hope

Begin this day with a genuine Thank You. Pray that you walk
with only a kind word. Step with the rhythm of peace. Breathe
deeply and honor our Creator with your good thoughts and
gratitude through the day.

Offer the gift of patience to yourself and all others with respect.
Allow yourself to be an instrument of hope, healing
and mercy!

Overstanding

I may not understand each circumstance,
or reason why,
but I stand with you.

I will be there as your friend if you desire, in the both the calm
and the storms of life.

We may travel different paths
or dis-agree in the moment
but somewhere in the Universal loop of overstanding—
what has always been
and will always be is my hope and appreciation
for you and your unique journey.

What is overstanding?
Overstanding is the gift of love
without condition,
just because!

It is being able to speak from your heart
and say for all time,

"I Stand With You!"

Being Thankful, and Seeing G-D

Beloveds,

What do we have to be thankful for?

When we are alive,
we learn to be thankful
for every experience
that offers us a moment
to awaken within our hearts.

I invite you to join me
as I say thank you . . .

Thank You for each moment
of Loving Grace.

Thank you for each
learning opportunity which
calls for me to expand
and develop in deep understanding.

Thank you for each mistake
which has given me new wisdom.

Thank you for showing me true
compassion in the hearts of others,
as I learn to meet them heart to heart.

Thank you for my tears
which show me the unlimited
depth of my heart, much like
the vastness of your Uni-Verse.

Being Thankful, and Seeing G-D

Thank you for the disappointment
and hard lessons that allow me to learn
to release judgment and discover
new gifts because I am able to
let go of my expectations.

Thank you for allowing me
deep listening, as well as
an incomprehensible space
that leaves me with joy to share.

Thank you for the breath of
your Loving Grace, and your
constant Divine Whisperings
that resides within me
and All Others.

Thank you for every argument
and world tantrum that calls
for All of Humanity
to let go of our
selfishness and greed.

Today I let go of my attachment
to what I think I know.

As I awaken within Your Heart,
I embrace the unknown with
hope, infinite faith and
appreciation for each Miracle
of Life!

Wrongdoings

We must try to never loan our names
or participate knowingly in wrongdoings.

Listen to your heart.
Follow the path of integrity and love.

Sometimes when there is no peaceful,
positive resolution, it is better
to walk away graciously.

Be patience. Be hopeful.

Keep the bridge open and pray
for another's awakening
in compassionate understanding.

Truth will be revealed, eventually.

Right now re-member that Divine Spirit
is leading you and will give you
a better way to serve
with integrity and love!

Listen Up America!

Listen Up America! Your children are tired of politician-parents bickering. You are breaking their hearts. Children want their parents to have jobs so that they can eat and have a place to call home. Children want their grandparents to be cared for with respect and love.

Children want to honor their President, like all the other Presidents have been honored and see good conversations about peace, not wars that wound or kill their parents.

Children want to live in a beautiful world where we appreciate and share our resources as we honor the Earth.
Listen Up America! Your Children offer their hearts with love; desire a world of safety, loving peace and shared prosperity.
That is the real conversation!

Living Your Word

Yesterday will become today, tomorrow. Our commitments of cooperation rest within our hearts waiting to be realized. How do we allow our word to become truth? How will we live the commitments we made yesterday? Today is the day to awaken the commitments in your heart. Each step you take with care, honor, dignity and mercy will allow you to live your words of compassion and realize your commitment of cooperation and hope. Yesterday's Truth Awaits. **Begin Today!** Live Your Word. Continue Tomorrow!

Savor the Promise

Day and Night promised to cherish each other and honor the greatness of the Uni-Verse. They see each other only at Dusk and at Dawn but the memory of their union grows and rests in the heart of the Sun and the Stars. All savor the promise and hope of each moment in time.

When we lovingly keep our word, we too honor Love's song. We savor the promise by offering our hearts and taking each breath in love!

What promises have you have made in love?
How are they cherished and being fulfilled within the Heart and Hope of the Uni-Verse?

What Do You Teach?

The good we share; the joy we emanate; the mercy and patience we offer; the care, understanding, respect and love we give are all observed, processed, recorded and remembered by our children. **Our children watch how we treat others, and then when we are old and in need of loving care, that is how they treat us! How kind are you to others? How do you embrace the infinite love of Divine Spirit?** What lessons are teaching your Children?

Wounded Healers

In some way, we have all been wounded
or wounded another.

Our purpose is not to hold anger or retaliate.

Our purpose is to learn forgiveness, to love
and to heal ourselves.

As we do good, and help others heal
we become wounded healers.

Our most precious jewels
then become our acts of love.

Thus we are able to live a life
of compassion and peace.

What acts of love will you share today?

Goodbye in Gratitude

There will be those to whom you open your heart and extend a hand of mercy, compassion and love. Do this always willingly. Even Strangers may truly appreciate and honor your efforts. There will be others who constantly call upon you and expect your gifts at every turn of their lives but will walk away when you are in need. Be prepared.

When they leave, say **Goodbye in Gratitude**. Your broken heart has just been opened and is ready to receive the great love that is coming for you! **Pray, Pay Attention and Prepare in Gratitude!**

Our Spiritual Inheritance

For every Master with a Peaceful Heart who has ever lived,
there were greedy people standing with swords,
ready for combat.

With courage, bravery and a commitment to fulfilling an
inner vision offered by our Creator,
these Masters—Women and Men
lovingly walked with hope, shared
and taught the virtue and value
of the peaceful, giving heart.

The core of their good teachings rest
within every religion and cultural tradition.

Let us live the lesson and accept their gift
of their eternal wisdom.

For when we love, honor
and respect our world neighbors . . .

When we forgive and care for others
with grace and compassion . . .

Then, we will truly embrace Our Universal Spiritual Inheritance!

Our Promise

A very wise man was asked a question
and his answer was simply—
"Continue to share your love for life".

Therein lies the message of a deep Divine Gift.
Moment to moment, day by day, year by year,
we must promise ourselves
to try to see love in all
and share our love for life.

When we make this promise of love
we are given the gift of eternal hope.

And in trying to always share
our love for life,—

Love Itself,
becomes an infinite refuge
and a place of healing and peace.

What the Future Holds

In these days of harmonic dissonance,
we must be careful of what we say
and what we do.

Our sometimes venomous ideas
and violent arguments may backfire.

What may happen is this—the very people
we believe we despise today,
our daughters and sons will love tomorrow.

There is a strong possibility that in their love
they will betray our hate and marry those
we thought were our enemies.

Our children will have children
that we will learn to love
because some part of them is US.

And then there will be no enemy.

If this is so,
then isn't far easier to begin today
to offer others the love and compassion
we seek for ourselves?

Isn't this the way to experience
a vivid peace with hope
and true joy in our lifetimes?

What will You choose for your future?
To live alone with hate?
or . . . .
To be nurtured with loving respect
by your children and grandchildren?

Re-Calibrate

The heart that learns stillness
breathes deeply, re-calibrates
and re-members divine will.

The deeper the breath,
the more rooted we become;
and with sure footing as our hearts open—
more oxygen travels into our brain.
This gift of the breath and oxygen
allows our minds and hearts
to connect in clear diamond consciousness.

It is through our breath that we are able
to re-calibrate and as we become more aware,
we move forward into our destiny with ease.
The heart that learns stillness
breathes deeply and re-calibrates often.
This is the gift of Divine Grace.

A Wise Person

A wise person allows others the experience of using their voice
and their gifts. No one is insignificant. We must listen to others
and honor their gifts. Try to create a space where others feel their
contributions are worthy. We are here,
together learning to work, build consensus and live in community.
Remember You Are Wise!

Wait Until Ready

No matter how good our intentions, we must be careful not to force our lifestyle, our truth or wisdom on others.
If we do, they may resent us! Offer small portions with love, expect nothing. Share a little more. Embrace their response
with respect and love. Be patient. Wait until one is ready to accept your gift. **All will awaken in time**.

Free Will

Our Creator has given us free will but too many of us have
decided to impose our will on others.
We compete with each other and destroy all that is in our path.
Humility and goodness have
become signs of weakness.

Our world will only grow and thrive
through our willingness to compromise.

We must have some humility
and work to restore goodness.
Today, let's simply want and offer
to others the good we want for ourselves.
Honor the loving presence
of Our Creator in All!

Live With Grace

Thank you for your unique contributions
to healing our planet. In these transitional times,
it is important to feel connected to all that is,
and to re-member that we are not alone.

The trees and other plant life
that give us oxygen to breathe love, share joy.

Birds and other animals bring us Divine messages and support.
It is now that we too must find joy within our hearts and share
it with others.

I know from personal experience that sometimes our gifts may
be rejected.

Still as we give, GRACE moves through us and gives us courage
to give again, and again with more LOVE.

For many of us, the day to day concerns of life are very
challenging. Collectively, shadows of fear have gained an
unusual strength, and are creating havoc on our glorious
Earth=Heart.

Conflict, confusion, unnatural violence, and lack of appreciation
for each other have many of us,
even global leaders living in a state of anxiety.

Some are wearing fear as a second skin
and causing irreparable harm.
Others of us are carrying the pain and hurt of rejection.

We are all beings of LOVE.
It is time to release our mental swords of fear.
It is time to let go of past disappointments.

I ask each of you to release
your personal cloaks of fear and pain into the universe.
LET THEM GO NOW.

Live With Grace cont

As we are able to do this, JOY and innocence will move
through us as a Rainbow of Grace.

Whether or not we are aware, there is a tiny doorway waiting
for each of us to step through.

It is here, in this small opening of eternal light
that we can rediscover hope and align ourselves
with our true nature and a Divine Spirit.

It is time for us to organize our lives
with humility, compassion, loving kindness and creativity.

Right now, we each have the opportunity
to re-member our inherent wisdom.
We can use our intuition
by magnifying the mustard seeds of LOVE.

This will allow us to share our hope
and courage so that we are able to have right words,
and right actions for each personal, community or global
situation.

Let us each re-commit to creating a world of equity,
sustainability and peace. Let our individual joy and cooperation
act as beacons of light to assist others in regaining hope and
experiencing healing.

Let us each believe in our own inherent goodness without a
shadow of a doubt! For as we believe it—so it shall be!

It is within the miracle of LOVE that crystals reflect rainbows
of JOY! Let us live in the moment with appreciation, faith and
hope. Let us sing songs of compassion, walk with kindness,
understanding, and a dedicated spirit of LOVE.

Our Dreams Need Nurtured

Our dreams need to be cared for, nurtured, and loved!

Beloveds, our dreams can blossom in the garden of life.
To do so, dreams need to be cared for, nurtured, and loved.

We must tend to our dreams through the seasons . . . the
hibernating winter, the blossoming spring, the active summer
and the harvesting fall.

We must be willing to do the work to make our dreams a reality.
And though we may have individual success,
we must ask ourselves . . .

What is it we as a Human Collective are dreaming?
A world where we share and nurture the positive loving dreams
or a world of war and destruction?

John F. Kennedy, the 35th President said during his speech
to the UN General Assembly on September 25th in1961
"Mankind must end all wars or war will end mankind!"

Another great man, The Rev. Dr. Martin Luther King, Jr. used
this quote more than once to stir us into right action.
And though we have heard this message from virtually
every peacemaker across centuries—
We are at an impasse now, and have been for many years.

Our Dreams Need Nurtured Cont

We readily forge the path of destruction
with drones and military spending for Israel, Iraq and
Afghanistan but we don't keep our commitment to assist the
more than 15 million unemployed or our more than 1 million
Haitian neighbors still living in tents with limited access to
water, and electricity.

Oh, the challenges we face in Haiti, Gaza, India, Tibet, Sudan,
Nigeria, Greece, Mexico and on every continent.
There are many, challenges on Earth!!!!

What is the problem? Why are people suffering?
Simply our GREED.

We continuously need more—bigger and more which results in
creating an imbalance on Our Mother-Earth=Heart
and in her vast oceans and environ. Thus we have earthquakes,
hurricanes, famines and oil spills.

And there is something VERY unnatural about the child
that holds the AK-47 gun with pride and believes it offers
the same kind of security as a mother and father working
together in love.

Our Dreams Need Nurtured Cont

Oh—be still my heart!

Unless we change, the end is near

for all our technological advances cannot end

our predilection to violence.

And violence destroys—and will continue

to destroy the heart of humanity.

What can we do?

We can stop our greed,

open our hearts and share our resources.

We can love one another

& learn to forgive each other,

share with each other

and learn live in peace!

The Humanist

I strive to be a humanist,

to dismiss ignorance by extending love,

to walk with an open heart,

to believe in the goodness

of all people.

It is a difficult journey.

My love has often been

mistaken for naivete.

My heart has been unnecessarily pierced

with swords of fear.

Still I continue on my path

and learn to walk . . .

more judiciously.

This Day

Blessed Creator of All,
Thank you for this day . . .
for I have awakened filled
with your grace.

That in itself is a
reason for joy!

I ask that you guide me
so that my every word
and action is a reflection
of your goodness.

I ask for your forgiveness
if I falter.

I ask for your love so that
I have the strength and courage
to extend love in the face of greed
so that I serve only You
in every sentient being.

Today your light and love
pour through me and show me
the purpose of my life!

In Confusion

Rise up not with anger
but in loving patience.

With all the confusion,
—the big fights
and the "me first" shoves,
we must be the peace.

Breathe deeply.

Step aside or back gently,
with humble dignity.

Go within and pray
for divine guidance.

In confusion, be the calm
heart of reason that listens
and acts with compassion.

**Breathe deeply and focus
only on a loving,
peaceful outcome.**

Harmonics as a Gift of Love

Inspired by the teachings of Elizabeth A. Hin

First there is a gentle touch, then an embrace,
next a re-membering, and another, and another,
and another re-membering
until we fully awaken into compassion,
humility, hope, joy, patience,
and understanding,
embraced by Divine Grace & Love.
This is the dance, the song,
and the gift of love that each being has to share.

Perhaps then, for each of us, the true miracle lies in our
willingness to allow, appreciate, and honor the uniqueness, and
freedom of each sentient being to sing the song of their heart.
And these songs, so glorious, simple, and profound
create a new Harmonic Rhythm of Divine Grace
which gives us a pathway HOME.

Home is Heaven On Mother Earth.

Home allows us the gift of respecting the gardens of others,
admiring ALL soul vibrations; and creating our own melodies
which complement all others including . . .
the pitter-patter of raindrops falling,
the whistling leaves as the wind flows through,
the bubbling brooks, birds singing
dolphins, whales and sea lions calling
dogs barking; cats, cheetahs, and cougars mewling;

Harmonics as a Gift of Love Cont

wolves howling, bears, camels, giraffes and horses chuffing,
huffing and neighing. frogs croaking, fish swishing.

Every sentient being has a sound
that contributes to the Harmonics of Love into Infinity.

Silence too is a sound.
The beats of the Sun, the Moon and the Ocean
create the symphonic movements of Time.
The wind speaks through a gentle breeze that calms and
soothes, as well as through tornadoes, and hurricanes that join
with rain to announce Mother Earth's hurt and anger at our
disregard for our Oneness.

**Is it possible that we desire to journey into the pathway of
the Uni-Verse?**

When will we collectively awaken into attention
with a willingness to heal, to dance, to sing,
to receive, and give the gift of LOVE?

My Beloveds, the Conductor is waiting, the time
to join the Uni-Versal Orchestra is NOW.

While I Am Here

While I'm here, I want to live just in this moment with a smile of love; and if pain and sorrow come; I want to embrace my tears and let my heart heal of all the wounds I will have only just discovered.

Even then, I want to give the gifts of hope and love that forever fill my heart. While I'm here I want to breathe deeply and be inspired by learning mercy, and forgiveness as I Dream a World of Peaceful Prosperity for All.

And I know that in the twilight of my life,
one day I will bid you bye for now;
and dance across the ocean waves
before I walk on clouds,
and join the many before me who sing
and dance with a Heavenly Glow!

While I'm here,
I want to live and love . . .

The Healing Adagio . . .

Part Five

Especially For Children
With Love
From
Miss Mellie Rainbow

What We Teach As Children

As children at play

we laugh, cry,

fall down, get up,

get angry or frustrated,

forgive, forget,

hold hands and stay friends.

We promise we will live a good life,

play, study, learn, share,

be kind, use our gifts and Bring

Our Light to the World!

When Love Smiles

A Children's Story to Illustrate and Share

Once upon a time,

LOVE smiled

and one by one, all over the earth

people felt LOVE's happiness.

People began to remember

all the things they had forgotten

to care about.

They remembered the beauty

of the glistening sun

that made them warm.

And the bursting clouds

that brought rain

so that everyone and everything

had water to drink.

When Love Smiles Cont

It took a long time to remember

but they did.

People remembered the beauty

of all the flowers,

the plants and trees,

the insects,

birds in the sky

and animals who walked on earth.

People remembered

the magnificent fish in the ocean,

and they understood the mysteries of whales

and the dolphins that hold earth's memories.

They began to appreciate

the exquisite moon

and the sparkling stars

in the sky at night.

When Love Smiles Cont

Many people decided to become one with nature.

They began to remember to care about everything.

LOVE smiled.

One by one people felt LOVE's happiness.

The people were happy that LOVE was happy.

Then they began to remember more and more.

People remembered that it was good

to sometimes be silent.

And in their silence

they listened to God

and felt joy in their hearts.

Then people remembered their ancestors.

Some people were afraid and angry

about bad things that had happened long ago.

When Love Smiles Cont

But LOVE kept smiling

and one by one

people decided to forget their fear.

Then they decided to forget their anger.

It took a long time

but these people remembered to have courage.

They worked harder for peace on earth.

Finally, people of all cultures

decided to have the courage

to remember the love in their hearts.

They remembered to listen to eachother.

All people began to share more.

They shared their food,

their knowledge and their technology.

When Love Smiles Cont

People of all cultures began to fall in LOVE,

to marry and have children.

Other children who needed parents

were adopted.

So many children looked different

from their mothers and fathers.

But it didn't matter

because people decided

that the most important thing

was to have LOVE in their hearts!

LOVE smiled and smiled.

The people felt LOVE smiling

and joined together in the spirit of unity.

When Love Smiles _{Cont}

And then one by one,

all the people from different cultures and religions, all the

artists, musicians, scientists, teachers and leaders,

all the people in governments and corporations

began to build a rainbow bridge

across the earth.

LOVE was sooooo happy

And the people felt LOVE's joy!

Now grandparents and parents

teach children

that we are all one in LOVE's heart.

And through your eyes,

as you learn,

you teach grown-ups

to remember everything beautiful on the Earth.

When Love Smiles Cont

And together as we continue

to build our Global Family,

each day,

one by one

we decide to remember,

to feel more and more of LOVE's LOVE.

And LOVE smiles and smiles and smiles.

LOVE just keep smiling more every day!

Special Note

Please draw pictures of what

When Love Smiles means to you

and share this story with your families and friends!

We Are For World Change

Inspired by All the Children of the Earth

We Are For World Change! Change the World.
We are the children of hope and the mirrors of Love.
We Are For World Change! Change the World.
Let's Change the World!

I don't know how to help—or what I could dream.
The problems are big.
Do you know what I mean?

Global Warming and wars, with no food to share.
Earth equals Heart. Can we please learn to care?

We Are For World Change! Change the World.
We are the children of hope and the mirrors of Love.
We Are For World Change! Change the World.
Let's Change the World!

Violence is never right.
We've got to help make it end
Let's open our hearts and learn to be friends.

We are the children of hope, and mirrors of love.
And with the new day, we bring a new way . . . .

We Are For World Change Cont

We are asking our parents, our teachers
our artists, musicians and friends
our leaders, our scholars, and our diplomats
—the list never ends.

We Are For World Change! Change the World.
Food, Healthcare, Education and Housing for ALL.
Peace, Understanding, Compassion and Love.

We Are For World Change! Change the World.
Let's Change the World!

We are the children of hope and the mirrors of Love.

We represent the NEW DAY
And with the new day, We Bring A New Way . . . .
Peace, Sharing, Understanding, Compassion, and
Love.

Let's Change the WORLD!
We Are the Children of Hope
and the Mirrors of Love!

We Are For World Change

What Can Children Do To Help Change The World?

Ask parents, grandparents, aunts, uncles, cousins, brothers, sisters and friends to help.

Have fun, study, develop and use your gifts help others and learn to be responsible.

Have book sales, bake sales, lemonade and yard sales to raise money to help people who are sick, poor or homeless.

Walk with an open heart. Be hopeful!

Be kind to each other even if someone is different.

Learn and teach other people about global warming.

Recycle to help save our Earth.

Write poems or stories and draw pictures that show how to help others. Share books and toys.

Become diplomats, and talk about Peace, Sharing, Understanding, Compassion, and Love.

Be a Mirror of Love!

When People Are Unkind
A Heart Song to Share

If you listen carefully and sing this song, you
will feel that only love belongs . . . .

When people, people are unkind,
never you mind, never you mind.

They may say hurtful things,
cause fear rules their hearts.

Life for them may seem like it's
been falling apart.

Love them anyway, love them anyway.

You can show them the way.
Be your best in every way, everyday!

Just believe . . . believe in yourself, because with your good
deeds and thoughts, there's no anger to be bought, no fear to be
taught.

You are given joy and peace of mind, when no matter
what,—you remember to be kind!

When People Are Unkind Cont

When people, people are unkind,
never you mind.

You have the strength and courage to live this day in Grace.

Every word you say,
every step you take,
can one day benefit the Hue-Man Race.

When people, people are unkind,
never you mind.

Love them anyway, love them anyway.
Show them the way.

Be your best every day,
in every way!

You can help save the Hue-Man Race each time you take a step
in Grace.

When people are unkind,
never you mind!

Cause you listened carefully, and you know this song. Now you
know that only love belongs! You can help save the Hue-Man
Race each time you take a step in Grace.

About the Author

Melony McGant is a poet, humanist and compassionate **communications professional with more than 20 years experience in assisting both people and organizations discover and promote their professional or personal life missions. She has a** strong track record of success in public relations, cause marketing and special events programming. Melony is also an ordained Interfaith Minister, a professional storyteller and author of the novel "**Sunshine & Olivier**: *A Parable of Love*. A member of *the American Academy of Poets* and the *Poetry Society of America*, her work included in several anthologies, including The **Book of Hope** and **The World Book of Healing (**both by Beyond Borders Press), and **Go Tell Michelle**: *African American Women Write to Michelle Obama* (SUNY Press).

Front Cover photo by Tyrone Rasheed

To Contact:

Melony McGant aka Miss Mellie Rainbow

P.O. Box 230103

New York, NY 10023

212-502-0895

Email: melonymcgant@yahoo.com

www.melonymcgant.blogspot.com

end

I offer my sincere thanks and appreciation to the AuthorHouse Team: Kathryn Schwoerer, Crystal Tura, Evan Villadores, Alessandre Galen for the cover design, Neil Gerson and Edward Enriquez for the interior design and Johnathan Estes!   Thank you for meeting me heart to heart!